Activity Book

Caroline Nixon and Michael Tomlinson

CAMBRIDGE
UNIVERSITY PRESS

Map of the book

	Vocabulary	Grammar	Cross-curricular	Skills
Hello Page 4	Main character names Numbers Colors	**Greetings and introductions** *What's your name?* *I'm Henrietta.* *How old are you?* *I'm three.*		
1 Our new school Mission: Make our classroom English Page 6	Classroom objects and people Extension of classroom objects Sounds and spelling: *p, b*	**Where … ?** **Prepositions *in, on, under, next to*** *Where's the crayon?* *It's on the desk.* **Singular and plural nouns** ***this/these*** *What's this?* *It's a window.* *What are these?* *They're windows.*	*Be kind at school* Learn about being kind to classmates	Literature *The first day* A play script Reading and Writing Speaking
2 All about us Mission: Make an *All about me* book Page 18	Family Parts of the body Sounds and spelling: *th, t*	***is/are*** *Who is she?* *She's Jenny. She's a girl.* *Who is he?* *He's Jim. He's a boy.* **have / don't have** *I have brown hair.* *They don't have green eyes.* *Do you have red hair?* *Yes, I do. / No, I don't.*	*Using our senses* Learn about the five senses and sense organs	Literature *Sara's favorite game* A real-life story Reading and Writing Speaking
Review units 1–2				
3 Fun on the farm Mission: Make a farm Page 30	Farm animals Adjectives Sounds and spelling: *c, k, ck*	***is/are* + adjective** **adjective + noun** *He's a nice cat.* *They aren't old chickens.* **has / doesn't have** *It has long ears.* *It doesn't have small feet.* *Does it have a long face?* *Yes, it does. / No, it doesn't.*	*What do animals give us?* Learn about animal products	Literature *How cows got their spots* A fantasy story Reading and Writing Speaking
4 Food with friends Mission: Organize a picnic Page 44	Food and drink Extension of food and drink Sounds and spelling: *a*	**like / don't like** *I like chocolate.* *Harry doesn't like chocolate.* *Do you like chocolate?* *Yes, I do. / No, I don't.* **Making requests and offers** *Can I have some chocolate, please?* *Here you are.* *Would you like some ice cream?* *Yes, please. / No, thank you.*	*Making a recipe* Learn about ingredients and methods of cooking	Literature *A picnic with friends* A real-life story Listening Speaking
Review units 3–4				

	Vocabulary	Grammar	Cross-curricular	Skills
5 **Happy birthday!** Mission: Have a present-giving party Page 56	Toys Extension of toys Sounds and spelling: *h*	*whose ... ?* **Possessive** *'s* **Possessive adjectives** *my, your, his, her, our, their* *Whose bike is this? It's Jim's bike. His bike's orange.* *want/wants* *Does he want a teddy bear? Yes, he does. / No, he doesn't. What does he want? He wants a helicopter.*	*Shapes around us* Learn about shapes	Literature *The twins and their robots* A real-life story Listening Speaking
6 **A day out** Mission: Plan a wildlife tour Page 68	Vehicles and places Zoo animals Sounds and spelling: *ai, a–e*	*there is/are* *There's a car. There aren't any stores. Are there any animals? Yes, there are. / No, there aren't.* *Let's ...* *Let's play a game. That's a good idea.*	*Animals in the wild* Learn about animal habitats	Literature *When we go to the zoo* A poem Reading Speaking
Review units 5–6				
7 **Let's play!** Mission: Plan a sports day Page 82	Sports and hobbies Sports verbs and extension of sports Sounds and spelling: *s*	**Present progressive** *What are you doing? I'm riding a horse. What's she doing? She's swimming. Are they washing the car? Yes, they are. / No, they're not.* *can* **for permission** *Can we play tennis? Yes, you can, but you can't play here.*	*Look after your body!* Learn about how we can keep our bodies strong	Literature *A good friend* A real-life story Listening Speaking
8 **Around the house** Mission: Invite a friend to my house Page 94	Rooms and objects in the house Extension of objects in the house Sounds and spelling: *i*	*can* **for ability** *I can swim. He can't sing. Can you ride a horse? Yes, I can. / No, I can't.* **Prepositions** *in front of, between, behind* *There's a small rug in front of the armchair.*	*Houses around the world* Learn about different kinds of houses around the world	Literature *The clock on the wall* A poem Listening Speaking
Review units 7–8				
9 **Vacation time** Mission: Go on a vacation Page 106	Clothes At the beach Sounds and spelling: *j, h*	**Imperatives** *Look at this T-shirt. Clean those shoes.* *like/enjoy* + **gerund** *me, too/so do I,* *I like flying my kite. So do I. I enjoy taking pictures.. Me, too.*	*What can we see on vacation?* Learn about features of natural landscapes	Literature *The monkey and the shark* A traditional story Reading and Writing Speaking
10 **Review Unit** Page 122	**Units 1–9**			
	Word Stack			

Hello

1 🎧 5.02 **Listen and number. Then color.**

red	green	yellow	black	white
1	☐	☐	☐	☐

pink	purple	orange	gray	blue
☐	☐	☐	☐	☐

2 **Answer and draw.**

What's your name?

How old are you?

I'm Jenny. I'm six.

I'm _____.

I'm _____.

1 🎧 5.03 **Listen and (circle) the number.**

1

2 (4) 6

2

1 3 9

3

2 5 7

4

4 8 10

5

5 7 9

6

3 8 10

2 **Write the words.**

1 3 t h r e e ☐☐☐☐☐ ☐☐☐

2 7

3 9

4 2 ☐☐☐

5 1 ☐☐☐

6 4 ☐☐☐☐

7 8  ☐☐☐☐☐

8 5 ☐☐☐☐

9 10 ☐☐☐

10 6 ☐☐☐

1 Our new school

My unit goals

Practice	Say and write	Learn to say
	 new words in English	in English

My mission diary

	Hooray!	OK	Try again
1			
2			
3			
★			

My favorite stage: _____

Go to page 134 and add to your word stack!

☐ I can name things in my classroom.

☐ I can understand colors.

☑ I can read classroom words.

☐ I can answer questions with *Where ...?*

1 Look and read. Write *yes* or *no*.

1 The chair is purple.   yes ✓

2 The desk is orange.   no ✓

3 The pen is green.   ~~Yes~~ no ✓

4 The crayon is blue.   yes ✓

5 The eraser is white.   no ✓

6 The bag is brown.   yes ✓

7 The book is red.   no ✓

8 The pencil is pink.   yes ✓

8/8

Sounds and spelling

2 🎧 5.04   **Listen and point to the letter. Then say and match.**

p or b?

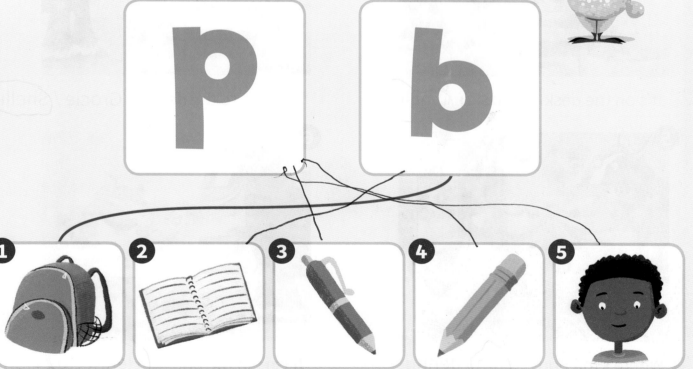

p   b

1   2   3   4   5

1 5.05 🎧 **Listen and read. Who says it? Circle the name.**

1

I'm the teacher.   (Gracie) / Cameron

2

It's under the desk, teacher.   Gracie / Rocky

3

It's on the desk.   Rocky / Shelly

4

It's next to the desk.   Gracie / Shelly

5

Where's my bag?   Jim / Jenny

6

It isn't in the bag.   Henrietta / Harry

1 🎧 5.06 Listen and put a check (✓) or an ✗ in the box.

2 Look at the picture. Complete the sentences.

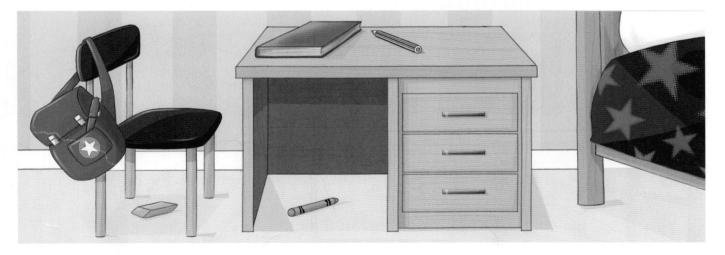

1 The book is ___on___ the desk.

2 The eraser is _____ the chair.

3 The pen is _____ the bag.

4 The pencil is _____ the book.

5 The crayon is _____ the desk.

6 The bag is _____ the chair.

1 Write the words. Find the secret word.

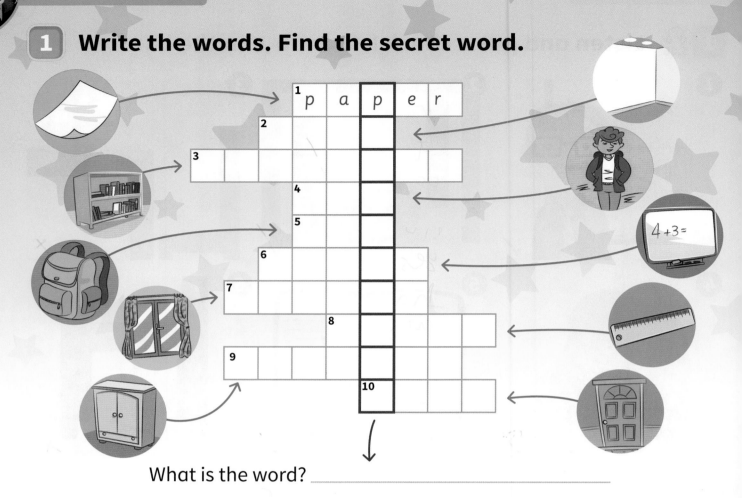

1. p a p e r
2.
3.
4.
5.
6.
7.
8.
9.
10.

What is the word? _____

2 🎧 5.07 Listen and draw lines.

1 🎧 5.08 Listen and number.

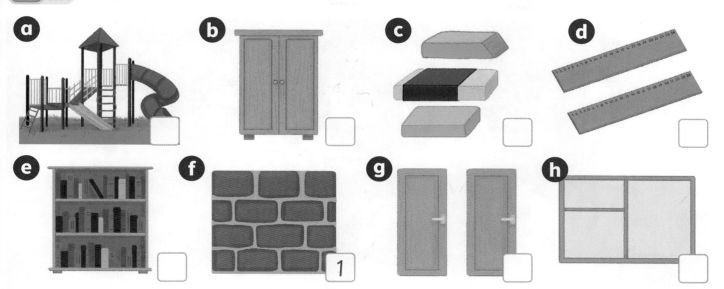

a

b

c

d

e

f `1`

g

h

2 Look and draw. Then write the words.

crayon   cabinet   It's   rulers   these   ~~this~~   this   window

1

A What's _____ *this* _____ ?

B It's a _____ .

2

A What's _____ ?

B It's a _____ .

3

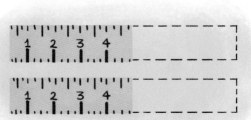

A What are _____ ?

B They're _____ .

4

A What's this?

B _____ a _____ .

1 **Who is kind? Look and (circle).**

2 **Look and write the words.**

~~Are you OK?~~   Here you are.
Thank you.   Yes, thank you.

1 Are you OK?

3 How are you kind at school? Write the words.

help   listen   ~~share~~   work

1

I ___*share*___ my things.

2

I _____ to my classmates.

3

I _____ my classmates.

4

We _____ together.

4 How are you kind at home? Think and draw.

1 **Listen and draw.**

2 **What do you take to school? Complete the rhyme.**

Take _____*a pencil*_____ to school – that's the rule.

Take _____ to school – that's the rule.

Take _____ to school – that's the rule.

Take _____ to school – that's the rule.

3 🎧 5.10 **Listen, point, and draw lines.**

4 **Look and point. Ask and answer.**

What's this? It's a bookcase.

What color is it? It's green.

1 Look and read. Put a check (✓) or an X in the box. There are two examples.

Examples

 This is a crayon. ✓

 These are chairs. X

Questions

1 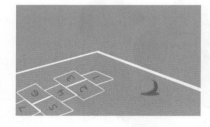 This is a playground. ☐

2 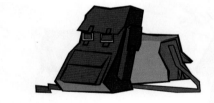 These are bags. ☐

3  This is a door. ☐

4  This is a pencil. ☐

5  These are erasers. ☐

1 **Play the game.**

What's this? | It's an eraser.

	What's this? 	What are these? 	Where's the pen? 	What are these? 

START

What's this?  | What's this?  | Where's the book?  | HAVE ANOTHER TURN | MISS A TURN

What's this?  | HAVE ANOTHER TURN | What are these?  | What's this?  | Where are the rulers?

What's this?  | MISS A TURN | What are these? | What's this? | What are these?

HAVE ANOTHER TURN | Where's the board?  | What are these?  | What's this?  | What's this?

FINISH | What's this?  | What are these?  | Where's the paper?  | MISS A TURN

2 All about us

My unit goals

Practice	Say and write  new words in English	Learn to say in English

My mission diary

	Hooray!	OK	Try again
1			
2			
3			

My favorite stage: _____

Go to page 134 and add to your word stack!

I can talk about my family.

I can listen to a song and do the actions.

I can name parts of the body.

I can read sentences about a picture.

1 Look and say.

Sounds and spelling

How do we say these letters?

th t

2 🎧 5.11 🎧 5.12 Listen and repeat. Which words have these sounds? Listen and write *th* or *t*.

1 mo _th_ er

2 ca __

3 fa __ er

4 bro __ er

5 grandfa __ er

6 sis __ er

7 grandmo __ er

1 **Read and put a check (✓) or an ✗ in the box.**

1 She's my mom. ✓

2 She's my sister. ☐

3 He's my brother. ☐

4 They're my brother and sister. ☐

2 **Who is in Rocky's family? Look and draw a (✓) or an ✗.**

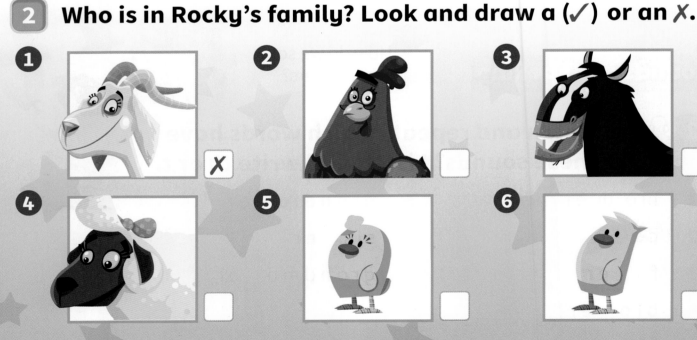

1 ✗

2 ☐

3 ☐

4 ☐

5 ☐

6 ☐

1 5.13 **Listen and follow. Draw lines.**

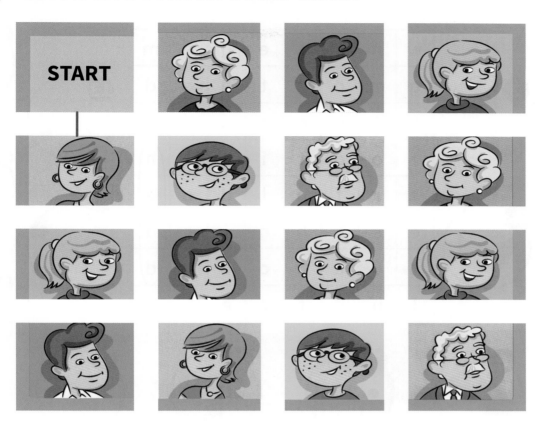

START

2 **Read and write.**

He's   He's   He's   He's   She's   She's   She's   She's

1    **2**    **3**    **4**

He's Ben.   _____ Kim.   _____ Tom.   _____ Ann.

_____ a boy.   _____ a girl.   _____ a boy.   _____ a girl.

1 Find and (circle) the words. Then write.

1 head

2

3

4

5

w	n	o	s	e	y	e	m
y	m	o	u	t	h	a	d
k	l	e	g	a	a	r	m
f	o	o	t	i	n	l	h
e	r	f	y	l	d	o	e
e	s	a	h	a	i	r	a
t	q	c	b	o	d	y	d
l	y	e	t	c	e	i	h

14

13

12

11

10

6

7

8

9

2 Write the words.

1  deah
h e a d

2 alit

3  byod

4  raih

5  tofo

6 sone

1 **Look and read. Write *yes* or *no*.**

Look at Hugo and Bill. They're cats.

1	They have gray faces.	_yes_	5	They have purple heads.
2	They have blue ears.	____	6	They have orange bodies.
3	They have red tails.	____	7	They have brown feet.
4	They have pink mouths.	____	8	They have yellow legs.

2 **Read and draw. Color.**

Hello. My name's Rob. I'm a robot. I have a yellow body and I have a blue head. I have orange arms and I have gray hands. I don't have a tail. I have green legs and my feet are black. My face is pink and I have two purple eyes. I have a gray nose and a brown mouth. I have two red ears, but I don't have hair.

have/don't have **23**

1 Look and write the words.

hear   see   smell   taste   ~~touch~~

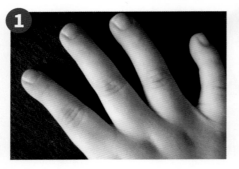
touch

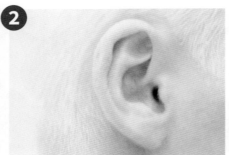

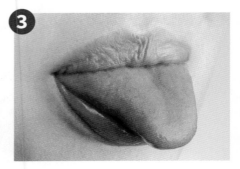

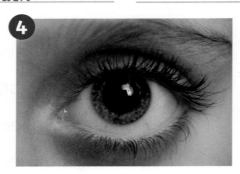

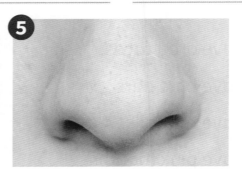

2 Which sense are they using? Look and color the T-shirts.

 hear   see   smell   taste   touch

Learn about the five senses and sense organs

3 Which senses do you use when you do these things? Read, think, and check (✓).

	I see	I hear	I smell	I taste	I touch
eat a sandwich					
watch TV					
play with a pet					

4 Think of something you do at home. Draw it and check (✓) the senses you use.

1 Number the sentences in order.

a   Sara is in the cupboard. ___

b   Sara is under the table! ___

c   Pablo and Sara play *Hide and Seek*. _1_

d   Sara isn't in the yard. ___

e   Sara isn't in the cupboard. ___

f   Sara isn't next to the bookcase. ___

2 Draw Pablo in the picture. Play "Where's Pablo?"

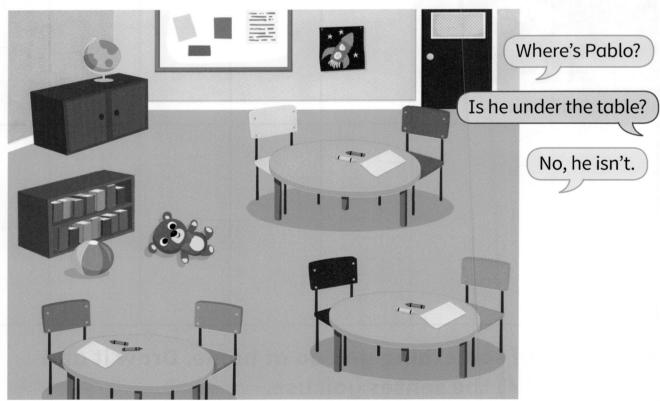

3 **Which body part can you see? Write the words.**

1

anhd

h a n d

2

deha

— — — —

3

ysee

— — — —

4

tefe

— — — —

5

riah

— — — —

6

tmuho

— — — —

4 **Look and point. Ask and answer.**

What's this?

It's a hand.

What are these?

They're eyes.

1 Look and read. Write *yes* or *no*.

Examples

Grandpa has gray hair.	yes
The pencil is on the chair.	no

Questions

1   The cat has white feet. _____

2   Dad is next to a desk. _____

3   Mom is reading a book. _____

4   The cupboard is under the window. _____

5   There's a blue ruler in the bag. _____

1 Play the game.

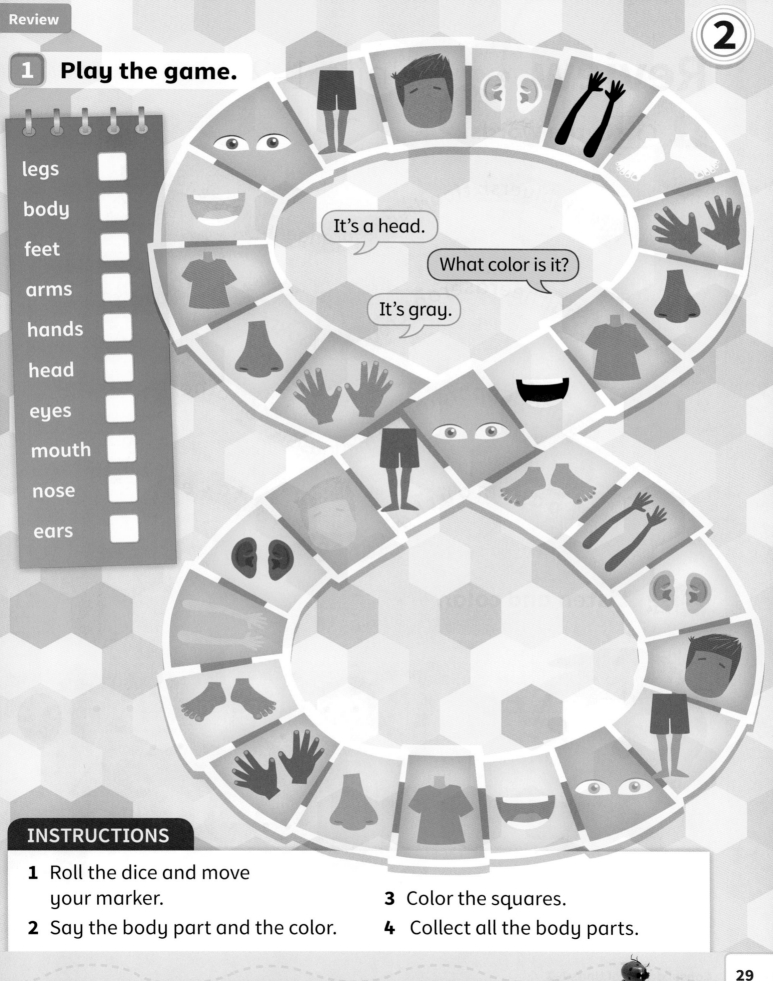

legs
body
feet
arms
hands
head
eyes
mouth
nose
ears

It's a head.

What color is it?

It's gray.

INSTRUCTIONS

1 Roll the dice and move your marker.

2 Say the body part and the color.

3 Color the squares.

4 Collect all the body parts.

Review ••• Units 1–2

1 (Circle) the words.

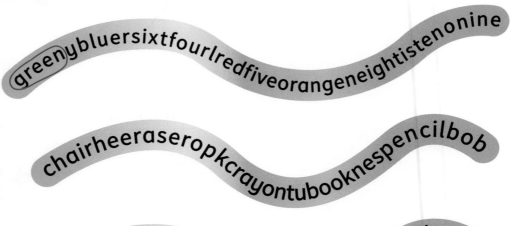

greenybluersixtfourlredfiveorangeneightistenonine

chairheeraseropkcrayontubooknespencilbob

grandpappbrothertfatherlqusistersomotherwi

headermouthyeyesepfeetobfaceas

2 🎧 5.14 **Listen and color.**

3 **Ask and answer.**

	Name: _____	Name: _____	Name: _____	Name: _____
Do you have black hair?				
Do you have brown eyes?				
Do you have a cat?				
Do you have a dog?				
Do you have a ruler?				

Do you have black hair? No, I don't.

4 **Look at Activity 3. Write about you.**

1 I have _____ hair.

2 I have _____ eyes.

3 I _____ a cat.

4 I _____ a dog.

5 I have _____, _____,

   and _____ in my *school bag*.

3 Fun on the farm

My unit goals

Practice	Say and write	Learn to say
	8 10 12	
	new words in English	in English

My mission diary

	Hooray!	OK	Try again
1	😊	😐	😕
2	😊	😐	😕
3	😊	😐	😕
★	😊	😐	😕

My favorite stage: _____

Go to page 134 and add to your word stack!

I can name farm animals.

I can talk about animals and people.

I can spell animal words.

I can write about what animals give us.

1 Count and write.

cats   chickens   cows   dogs   donkeys
ducks   goats   ~~horse~~   sheep

I can see one ¹___horse___, two ²_____, three ³_____,
four ⁴_____, five ⁵_____, six ⁶_____,
seven ⁷_____, eight ⁸_____ and nine ⁹_____.

Sounds and spelling

2 🎧 5.15 **Can you hear the /k/ sound?**
Listen and say *yes* or *no*.

3 🎧 5.16 **Listen and color the letters that**
make the /k/ sound.

How do we
write that
sound?

1

2

3

4

5 cow

The Friendly Farm

1 **Read and write a check (✓) or an ✗ in the box.**

1

Rocky's new friend is a spider. ✓

2

Harry's a small horse. ☐

3

Cameron's a long cat. ☐

4

Rocky's brother and sister are old. ☐

5

Gracie's young. ☐

6

Cameron's short. ☐

2 **Talk about the animals. Use the words in the box.**

big   small   long   short   old   young   nice

Harry's big.

Story: *is/are* + adjective and adjective + noun in context

1 Read and color.

The small horse is black.
The long pencil is blue.
The young cat is orange.
The big duck is yellow.
The new book is green.
The short ruler is purple.
The old cat is gray.

2 Write the words in the correct order.

1 short / The sheep have / tails / .   *The sheep have short tails.*

2 spider / a small / It's / .

3 nice / They're / ducks / .

4 is big / horse / The / .

5 cats / They're / old / .

6 The donkeys have /
   ears / big / .

7 young / small and / I'm / .

1 Read and (circle) the correct words.

1 It's a **sad** / **happy** cat.

2 It's an **ugly** / **beautiful** spider.

3 It's an **angry** / **nice** donkey.

4 They're **happy** / **sad** sheep.

5 They're **beautiful** / **ugly** ducks.

6 It's a **funny** / **angry** goat.

2 Write the words.

> angry   beautiful   funny   happy   ~~nice~~   sad   ugly

1 This is the Mutt family. It's a family of dogs. They're _n i c e_.

2 The grandfather is __ __ __ __ __ __.

3 The mother is
__ __ __ __ __ __ __ __ __.

4 The brother is __ __ __ __ __.

5 The grandmother is __ __ __ __ __.

6 The father is __ __ __ __ __.

7 The sister is __ __ __.

1 🎧 5.17 Listen and check (✓).

1 Which horse does Tom think is beautiful?

A  ✓
B
C

2 Who is May?

A
B
C

3 What's in Alex's school bag?

A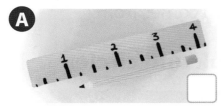
B
C

4 Which cat is under Jill's chair?

A
B
C

5 Which robot is in the picture?

A
B
C

6 Which animals does Dan have on his farm?

A
B
C

1 **Which animal does it come from? Read and write.**

bees   chickens   ~~cows~~   sheep

1   Milk comes from __cows__ .

2   Eggs come from _____ .

3   Honey comes from _____ .

4   Wool yarn comes from _____ .

2 **Which things come from animals? Look and circle.**

3 Read the sentences. Number the pictures in order.

1   This is an alpaca. It has a lot of wool.

2   People cut the wool.

3   They make balls of wool yarn in different colors.

4   They use the yarn to make clothes.

1

4 What things from animals do you have at home? Think and draw.

1 **Read the sentences. Number the pictures in order.**

1   The flies bite Cathy.

2   Little Horse and Cathy jump in the mud.

3   The young cows laugh at Cathy.

4   Cathy is black and white. The flies don't bite her.

a

b

c

d

2 **Read and write. Then write and draw.**

1   Cathy is scared of _____ .

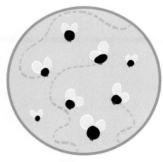

horses   flies   spiders   mud

2   I am scared of

_____ .

3 **Look and read. Write *yes* or *no*.**

1	There are fourteen animals.	no
2	The animals are in a classroom.	
3	Cathy is a white cow.	
4	There are four sheep.	
5	There are four cows.	
6	The horses are smiling.	
7	Cathy's mom is looking at Cathy.	

1 Look at the pictures. Look at the letters. Write the words.

Example

_c_ _o_ _w_

Questions

1

_ _ _ _ _ _ _

2

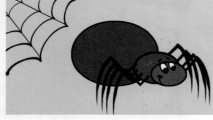

_ _ _ _ _ _

3

_ _ _

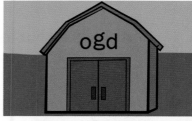

4

_ _ _ _ _

5

_ _ _ _

1 Play the game.

START

long

new

happy

angry

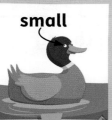
small

young

happy

big

small

long

big

old

ugly

short

young

long

sad

sad

young

big

beautiful

beautiful

big

funny

FINISH

angry

short

funny

nice

The duck has small eyes.

The duck is young.

INSTRUCTIONS

1 Roll the dice and move your marker.
2 Look at the picture and read the word. Say a sentence.

4 Food with friends

My unit goals

Practice	Say and write	Learn to say
	⭐ 8 ⭐ 10 ⭐ 12 new words in English	in English

My 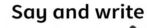 diary

	Hooray!	OK	Try again
①			
②			
③			
⭐			

My favorite stage: _____

Go to page 134 and add to your word stack!

☐ I can ask and answer questions with *Would you like … ?* and *Can I have … ?*

☐ I can listen and write what food people like.

☐ I can listen and choose the correct picture.

☐ I can talk about food and drink.

1 Write the words.

 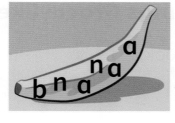 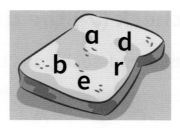 

1 ___mango___ 2 b_____ 3 b_____ 4 h_____

5 c_____ 6 c_____ 7 s_____ 8 w_____

Sounds and spelling

How do we say this letter?

2 🎧 5.18 🎧 5.19 Listen and say. Then listen and match.

mango

cake

1  salad

2  cat

3  paper

4  lemonade

5  bag

The Friendly Farm

1 **Read and check (✓) the things Gracie likes.**

I like cake, bananas, bread, socks, and books!

 ✓

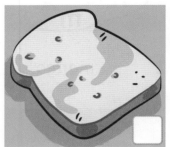

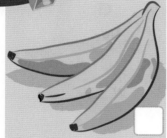

2 🎧 5.20 **Listen and match the animals to the things they like.**

 1

 2

 3

 4

Story: *like / don't like* in context

(4)

1 Read and circle.

1 I **like** / **don't like** bread.

2 I **like** / **don't like** chicken.

3 I **like** / **don't like** bananas

4 I **like** / **don't like** lemonade.

5 I **like** / **don't like** water.

6 I **like** / **don't like** cake.

7 I **like** / **don't like** salad.

8 I **like** / **don't like** mangoes.

2 Read and match. Color.

He doesn't like milk.

She doesn't like hamburgers.

He likes salad.

He doesn't like cats.

She likes bananas.

She likes school.

1 Look and read. Put a check (✓) or an ✗ in the box.

1 These are meatballs. ✗

2 These are oranges. ☐

3 These are sausages. ☐

4 This is fruit. ☐

5 These are beans. ☐

6 These are lemons. ☐

7 This is juice. ☐

8 These are grapes. ☐

2 Write the word and ask your friend. Put a check (✓) or an ✗ in the box.

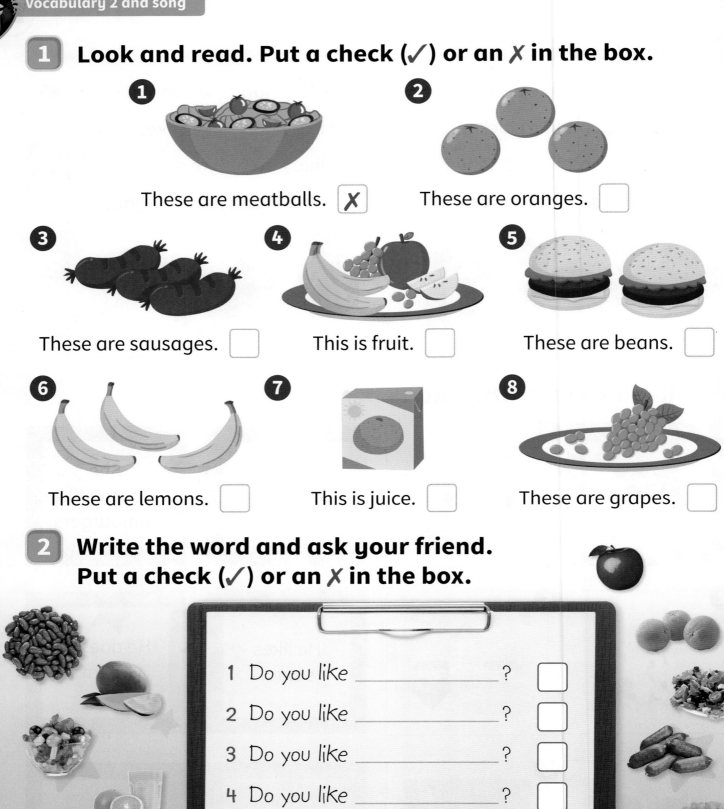

1 Do you like _____ ? ☐

2 Do you like _____ ? ☐

3 Do you like _____ ? ☐

4 Do you like _____ ? ☐

5 Do you like _____ ? ☐

6 Do you like _____ ? ☐

1 Read and complete. Then draw and write.

~~bread~~   hamburger   Can   like   Would

1

A Can I have some ___bread___ ?

B Yes, here you are.

2

A Would you like a _____ ?

B No, thank you.

3

A _____ I have an apple, please?

B Yes, here you are.

4

A _____ you like some milk?

B Yes, please.

5

A Would you _____ some grapes?

B No, thank you.

6

A Can I have _____ , please?

B _____ .

1 Write the words.

> carrots   cheese   meat   onions
> ~~pasta~~   potatoes   rice   tomatoes

1

pasta

2

3

4

5

6

7

8

2 Match the ingredients to the dish.

1
Ingredients
Fruit:
apple
kiwi
mango
grapes

2
Ingredients
rice
meatballs
tomatoes
peas

3
Ingredients
meat
potatoes
tomatoes
peas

a

b

c

3 **Read the recipe and write the words.**

cheese   ~~eggs~~   eggs   omelet   onion   tomatoes

1 You need two ___eggs___ , some cheese, _____ , and an onion.

2 Mix the eggs. Cut the _____ and the tomatoes.

3 Cook the _____ for four minutes.

4 Put the _____ , onion, and tomatoes on the eggs.

5 Fold the _____ and cook it for one more minute.

4 **What would you like in your omelet? Draw and write.**

I'd like _____ in my omelet.

1 Find the words in the puzzle. Then check (✓) the things Matt and Mia take on their picnic.

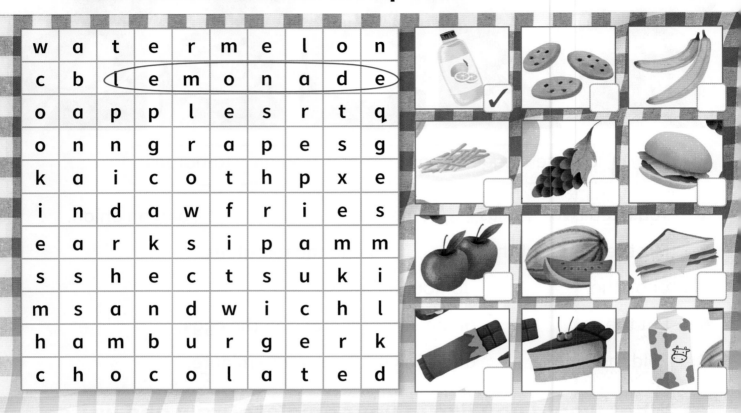

2 Put the pictures in order. Then tell the story.

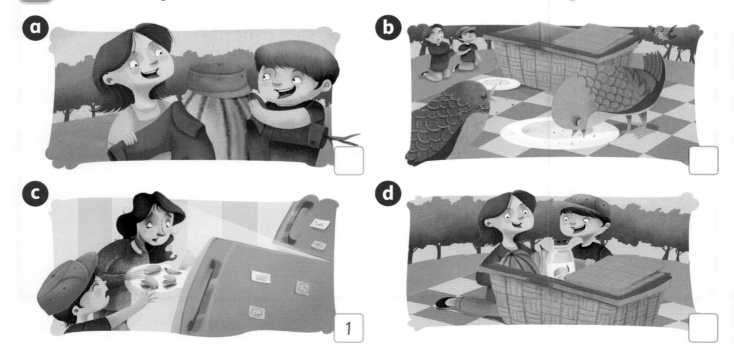

3 🎧 5.21 **Listen and draw lines from the names to the children in the picture.**

Matt   Mia   Tom

Tina   Sam   Harry

1 🎧 5.22 Look at the pictures. Listen and check (✓) the box. There is one example.

Which is Bill's sister?

A  ✓

B

C

1 How old is Anna?

A

B

C

2 Where's Matt's eraser?

A

B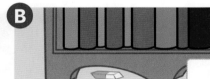

C

3 What are the new animals on the farm?

A

B

C

4 What would Sam like for lunch?

A

B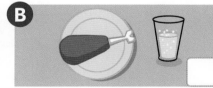

C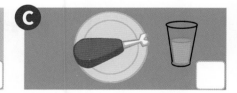

5 Which is Lucy's brother?

A

B

C

1 Play the game.

My shopping list

1 _____ ☐   3 _____ ☐   5 _____ ☐

2 _____ ☐   4 _____ ☐   6 _____ ☐

OPEN
START SHOPPING!

Can I have ...?

Can I have ...?

Can I have ...?

Can I have ...?

Can I have ...?

FINISH!

Would you like some lemonade?

Yes, please!

Can I have some oranges?

INSTRUCTIONS

1 Choose the food and drinks for your shopping list.

2 Roll the dice and move your marker.

3 Collect your food and drinks.

4 Go to the Finish! square.

Review • • • Units 3–4

1 Circle the words.

chickenlystspiderweuagoaterrtdonkeyednihorseoeld

changryriasbeautifulstlsfunnyopnosadheeruglyrkikjp

lemonadezyxwgrapesvutschocolaterqpobeansnmlkapple

jihgbananafedcakecbazfruityxwjuicetuvmangopopple

2 Read and match. Color.

He wants some
orange juice.

He doesn't want
any grapes.

She wants
some bananas.

3 **Write.**

~~angry~~   bread   cow   duck   hamburgers
happy   sad   salad   sheep

adjectives	food	farm animals
angry	_____	_____
_____	_____	_____
_____	_____	_____

4 **Look, read, and write.**

wool   meat   ice cream   butter   bees

We get a lot of things from animals. Honey comes from

(1) _____ . We get **(2)** _____ , milk, and

(3) _____ from cows. Eggs and **(4)** _____ come

from chickens. We get **(5)** _____ from sheep to make

sweaters and scarves.

5 Happy birthday!

My unit goals

Practice	Say and write	Learn to say
	8 10 12 new words in English	in English

My mission diary

	Hooray!	OK	Try again
1	:)	:|	:~
2	:)	:|	:~
3	:)	:|	:~
★	:)	:|	:(

My favorite stage: _____

Go to page 134 and add to your word stack!

I can talk about toys. ☐

I can ask and answer questions with *Whose ... ?* ☐

I can write a birthday card. ☐

I can understand letters of the alphabet that I hear. ☐

1 What is it? Look and write.

1  It's a bike.

2  _____

3 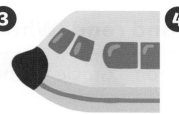 _____

4  _____

5  _____

6  _____

7  _____

8 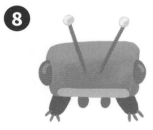 _____

Sounds and spelling

How do we say this letter?

2 🎧 5.23 **Listen and match the words to the pictures. Then listen again and say.**

a 　b 　c  1　d

1 house　　3 horse

2 happy　　4 hat

3 🎧 5.24 **Listen and say the rhyme.**

How is the **h**orse in **h**is little brown **h**ouse?

He's **h**appy in **h**is **h**at in **h**is **h**ouse with a mouse.

The Friendly Farm

1 🎧 5.25 **Listen and read. Who says it?**

| Cameron | Gracie | Gracie | Harry | Rocky | Shelly |

1 It's his favorite toy. ___Gracie___

2 Whose car is that? _____

3 Jim doesn't like dolls. _____

4 Jenny's favorite toy is her car. _____

5 Look at our birthday present for Jenny and Jim. _____

6 Oh, no! Not a plane! _____

2 **Read and correct.**

1 It's Rocky's birthday. It's Jim and Jenny's birthday.

2 Jenny's car is orange. _____

3 Jenny likes dolls. _____

4 Jim's favorite toy is his bike. _____

5 Their present is a ball. _____

6 Cameron likes planes. _____

1 Read and write *his*, *her*, or *their*.

It's Grandma and Grandpa's farm. It's _____*their*_____ farm.

They're Harry's feet. They're _____ feet.

It's Jenny's car. It's _____ car.

It's Jim and Jenny's house. It's _____ house.

They're Shelly's ears. They're _____ ears.

It's Grandpa's tractor. It's _____ tractor.

It's Grandma's plane. It's _____ plane.

They're Gracie's eyes. They're _____ eyes.

1 **Write.**

1 It's Nick's
_____toy box_____ .

2 It's Eva's
_____ .

3 It's Dan's
_____ .

4 It's Lucy's
_____ .

5 It's Ben's
_____ .

6 It's Anna's
_____ .

7 It's Alice's
_____ .

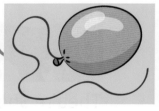

1   **Write *Yes, she does* or *No, she doesn't*.**

Pat's birthday list

* a new computer
* a red kite
* a board game
* a yellow robot
* a big teddy bear
* seven balloons
* a small radio
* a green ball

1   Does she want a new computer?   <u>Yes, she does.</u>

2   Does she want a red bike?   _____

3   Does she want a board game?   _____

4   Does she want a yellow robot?   _____

5   Does she want a small teddy bear?   _____

6   Does she want eight balloons?   _____

7   Does she want a big radio?   _____

8   Does she want a green ball?   _____

Write the words.

| circle | rectangle | square | ~~triangle~~ |

1  **2**  **3**  **4**

_____triangle_____ _____ _____ _____

 Which shapes can you see? Look and write.

1

2

I can see ____rectangles and circles____ . I can see _____ .

3

4

I can see _____ . I can see _____ .

3 **Read and draw the robot.**

His head is a big square.

His body is a triangle.

His two arms are rectangles.

His two hands are circles.

His two legs are circles.

His two feet are rectangles.

His nose is a triangle.

His eyes are small squares.

His mouth is a rectangle.

4 **How many shapes can you find at home? Count and write.**

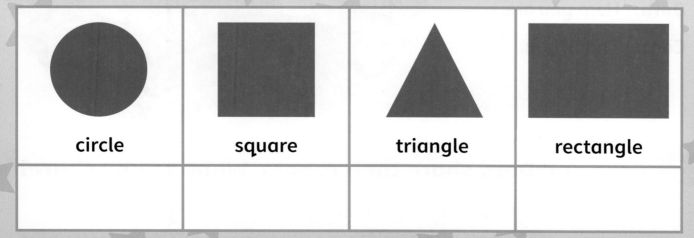

circle	square	triangle	rectangle

1 Read and write *yes* or *no*.

1   Dora and Cora are sisters. .... *yes* ....

2   Dora's favorite toy is a car. ....

3   Dora's robot is called Jill. ....

4   Cora gives her robot to Dora. ....

5   Cora and Dora are happy at the end of the story. ....

2 Choose Dora and Cora's toys and complete the dialog. Act it out with a partner.

Dora: Can I have your blue _____, please?

Cora: OK. Here you are.

Dora: Thank you! Can I have your _____ too, please?

Cora: Yes. Here you are.
            Can I have your red
            _____, please?

Dora: OK. Here you are.
            Would you like my
            _____?

Cora: Yes, please!

Dora: Here you are.

Cora: Thank you.

3 Cora and Dora share their robots. What do you share?

I share my toy plane with my brother.

4 Look and read. Put a check (✓) or an ✗ in the box.

1

This is Cora's helicopter. ✗

2

Dora has a red balloon. ☐

3

Dora's kite is blue. ☐

4

Cora has a ball. ☐

5

Dora has a car. ☐

6

This is Dora's teddy bear. ☐

1 🎧 5.26 Read the question. Listen and write a name or a number. There are two examples.

Examples

What is the name of Kim's doll?	Lucy
How old is the doll?	9

Questions

1	What's the name of Lucy's school?	_____ School
2	How many children are in Lucy's class?	_____
3	Who does Lucy sit next to?	_____
4	How many lessons does Lucy have today?	_____
5	What is the name of Lucy's teacher?	Mr. _____

5

1 Play the game.

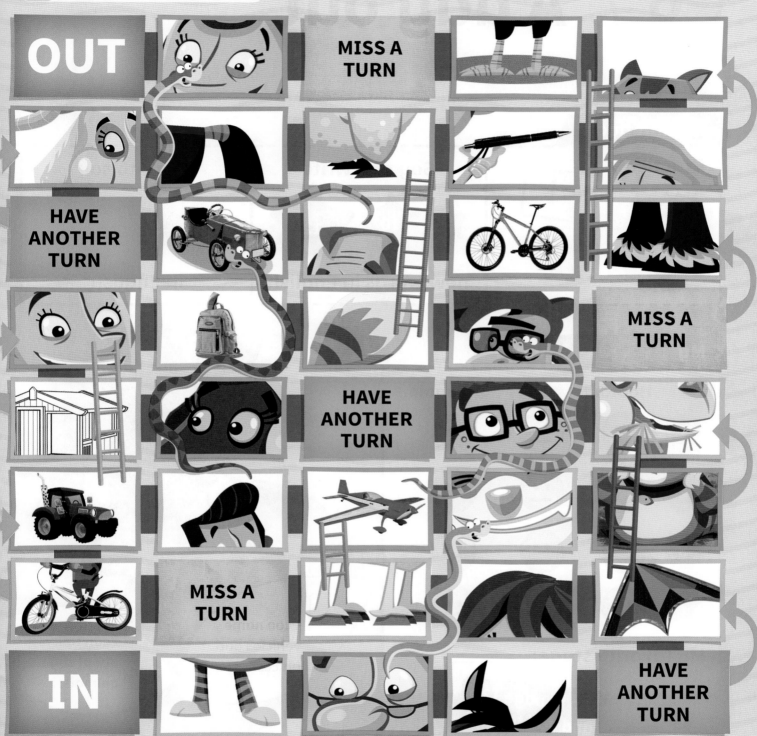

OUT

MISS A TURN

HAVE ANOTHER TURN

MISS A TURN

HAVE ANOTHER TURN

MISS A TURN

IN

HAVE ANOTHER TURN

INSTRUCTIONS

1 Roll the dice.
2 Move your marker.

3 What can you see?
Whose is it? Look and say.

It's Harry's tail.

6 A day out

My unit goals

Practice	Say and write  8 10 12 new words in English	Learn to say in English

My mission diary

	Hooray!	OK	Try again
1			
2			
3			
★			

My favorite stage: _____

Go to page 134 and add to your word stack!

☐ I can name vehicles and places.

☐ I can talk about zoo animals.

☐ I can understand a poem.

☐ I can read sentences and copy English words.

(6)

1 🎧 5.27 **Where are they? Listen and match.**

1	cat	d	4	Bill	☐	7	Lucy	☐	10	Jill	☐
2	Dan	☐	5	horse	☐	8	dog	☐			
3	Alice	☐	6	Mark	☐	9	Hugo	☐			

a park

b yard

c tree

d flowers

e bookstore

f car

g train

h motorcycle

i bus

j truck

Sounds and spelling

How do we write that sound?

2 🎧 5.28 **Listen and point. Then listen again and say.**

3 🎧 5.29 **Listen again and color the letters that make the /eɪ/ sound.**

train tail

cake plane table grapes

The Friendly Farm

1 🎧 5.30 **Listen, read, and write the number.**

a. There's a big truck. _____

b. There are old cars and motorcycles. _1_

c. There are flowers for Grandpa's new garden. _____

d. Are there new animals? _____

e. There aren't any new animals. _____

f. There's a truck and animals! _____

2 **What's in the truck? Look and put a check (✓) or an ✗.**

1. ✗
2.
3.
4.
5.

1 Read and color.

Look at the street. In the street, there's a purple car and a big blue truck. There's a red bus stop next to the truck.

Look at the store. There are two trains in the window. The big one's green, and the small one's brown. There's a park next to the store. In the park, there are three yellow flowers and a big green and brown tree.

2 Draw two more things in the picture. Listen to your friend and draw.

There's a brown dog in the park.

Is it next to the tree?

Yes.

1 Write the words.

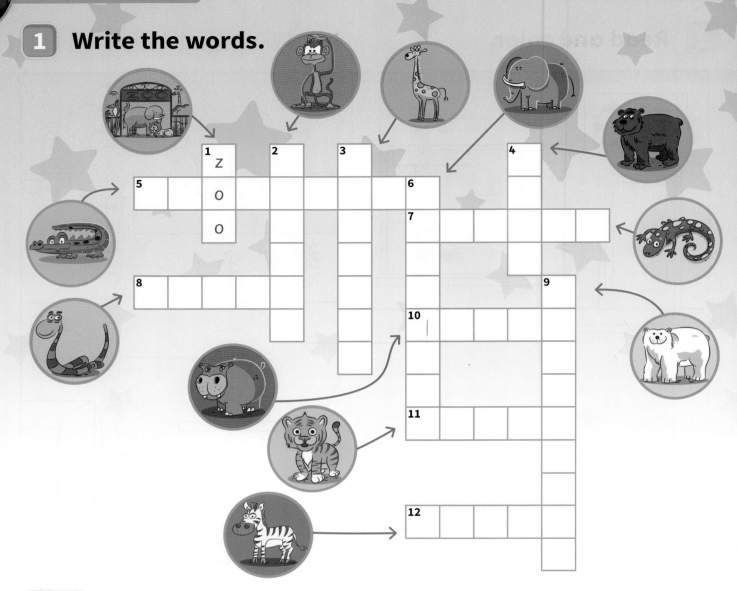

2 🎧 5.31 Listen and write a name or a number.

1 What is the girl's name? _____May_____

2 How old is the girl? _____7_____

3 How many monkeys do they have? _____

4 What's the small monkey's name? _____

5 How old is the young monkey? _____

6 What's Matt's father's name? _____

7 How old is Matt's father? _____

1 Read and write the words.

close   door   ~~boardgame~~   Let's   Let's   listen

Let's play a _____boardgame_____ .   _____ read a book.

Let's open the _____ .   _____ draw a picture.

Let's _____ the window.   Let's _____ to the radio.

1 Which animals live in the wild? Look and check (✓).

1 whale ✓

2 zebra ☐

3 dog ☐

4 jellyfish ☐

5 monkey ☐

6 fish ☐

7 giraffe ☐

8 penguin ☐

9 chameleon ☐

10 polar bear ☐

2 Where do the wild animals live? Write the words.

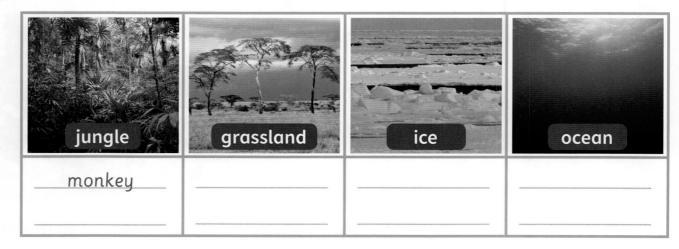

jungle	grassland	ice	ocean
monkey			

3 Read about the animals. Write the words.

> big ~~frog~~ meat rhino small
> snakes spiders trees water

This is a ¹ _frog_ . It is
² _____ and green.
It lives on land and in the
³ _____ . It can swim and
jump. In the wild, ⁴ _____
eat frogs and frogs eat flies and
⁵ _____ .

This is a ⁶ _____ . It
is ⁷ _____ and gray.
It can walk and it can swim,
too. It doesn't eat
⁸ _____ . It eats
⁹ _____ and flowers.

4 Choose an animal to learn about. Draw and write.

- elephant • tiger • lizard • polar bear

This is _____ .
It is _____ .
It lives in _____ .
It can _____ .
It eats _____ .

1 🎧 5.32 **Listen and number the animals in order.**

2 **Match the words that rhyme.**

day   tree   ~~zoo~~   zoo

1   do   _____zoo_____   3   play   _____

2   see   _____   4   too   _____

3 **Make your own zoo poem. Write the animals that you like at the zoo.**

I really like _____,
I like _____, too.
But I really love the _____,
When I go to the zoo.

4 🎧 5.33 Listen and point. Then draw lines.

5 Ask and answer.

What color is the …?

How many … are there?

Tell me about the …

Do you like …?

What's your favorite animal?

What color is the zebra?

It's black and white.

Tell me about the elephant.

It's big and gray.

1 **Read this. Choose a word from the box. Write the correct word next to numbers 1–5. There is one example.**

A zebra

Zebras are _____black_____ and white animals. They are like horses, but people don't ride them. A zebra's **(1)** _____ is nice and long. A zebra has four legs and two beautiful **(2)** _____. Lots of zebras live with their family. Some zebras live in the **(3)** _____. Zebras drink a lot of **(4)** _____, but they don't eat **(5)** _____.

Example

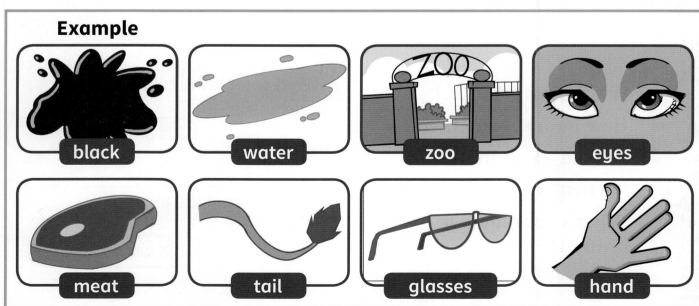

6

1 Play the game.

There are two hippos next to a bus stop.

FINISH

There's a zebra under the tree.

There are two monkeys in the helicopter.

There's a bear in the store.

There's a crocodile on the motorcycle.

There are three flowers on the truck.

START

There are two trees in the park.

There are two trees in the park.

INSTRUCTIONS

1 Roll the dice.
2 Move your marker.

3 Pictures: Say what you see.
4 Sentences: Read, find, and move to that square.

Review ••• Units 5–6

1 **Find three words in a line from the same group.**

1

doll	tree	flower
street	balloon	board game
computer	bus stop	kite

2

bus stop	lizard	bike
monkey	park	truck
giraffe	tiger	bookstore

3

keyboard	computer	truck
radio	train	bear
motorcycle	teddy bear	apple

4

park	house	polar bear
water	store	elephant
garden	donkey	hippo

2 🎧 5.34 **Listen and color.**

3 Write.

bear bus stop crocodile dog helicopter kite
lizard park plane robot store truck

places	transportation	wild animals	other
_____	_____	_____bear_____	_____
_____	_____	_____	_____
_____	_____	_____	_____

4 Read and match. Color.

They want a board game.

They don't want a teddy bear.

She doesn't want a beautiful doll.

7 Let's play

My unit goals

Practice

Say and write

8 10 12

new words in English

Learn to say

in English

My mission diary

	Hooray!	**OK**	**Try again**
1			
2			
3			
★			

My favorite stage: _____

Go to page 134 and add to your word stack!

I can talk about hobbies.

I can say what people are doing.

I can listen and find people in a picture.

I can understand questions with *Can I …?*

1 Read and match.

a Let's play basketball.

b Let's play the piano.

c Let's play soccer.

d Let's swim.

e Let's watch TV.

f Let's play tennis.

g Let's ride our bikes.

h Let's play the guitar.

Sounds and spelling

2 🎧 5.35 Listen and say the rhyme.

My **s**i**s**ter **S**ally likes **s**alad and **s**wimming, but I like **s**pider**s**, **s**au**s**ages, and **s**nake**s**!

How do we say this letter?

The Friendly Farm

1 **Read and circle the correct word.**

1

Tom's **riding** / **watching** Harry.

2

Rocky's brother and sister are **singing** / **eating**.

3

She's eating a **book** / **sock**.

4

She's painting her **face** / **feet**.

5

Rocky says he's playing **the guitar** / **the piano**.

6

Henrietta's **cleaning** / **painting** the barn.

2 **Look and talk about the people and animals. Use the words in the box.**

watching   riding   talking   walking   singing   smiling

Mr. Friendly is watching Tom and Harry.

Story: Present continuous in context

1 Look and read. Write *yes* or *no*.

1 The girl's driving a car. _no_

2 The baby's running. _____

3 The boy's playing tennis. _____

4 The mother's painting a picture. _____

5 The father's playing the guitar. _____

6 The grandfather's listening
to music. _____

2 Look and write the words.

am ~~are~~ aren't is isn't

A What _are_ you doing?

B I _____ listening to music.

A Are they playing basketball?

B No, they _____ .

A Is your mom watching TV?

B No, she _____ . She's reading.

A What's he doing?

B He _____ playing the guitar.

1 **Look and write the words.**

badminton   baseball   basketball   hitting
~~hockey~~   kicking   running   skateboard

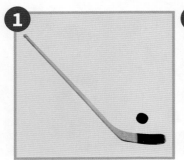
1

2

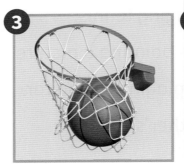
3

4

hockey

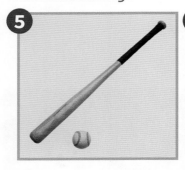
5

6

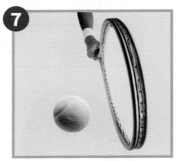
7

8

2 🎧 5.36 **Listen and color.**

1 Write the words in the correct order.

1

our skateboards / in the park / Can
we ride / ?

<u>Can we ride our skateboards</u>

<u>in the park?</u>

2

Can I throw / your dog / the ball for / ?

_____

_____

3

please / eat some cake, / Can we / ?

_____

_____

4

the train, / Can we go on / please / ?

_____

_____

5

Can I / please / watch TV, / ?

_____

_____

6

badminton in / the yard / Can we
play / ?

_____

_____

1 **Play a mime game. Do and say.**

> jump   run   stretch your legs
> stretch your arms   stretch your body

What am I doing?

You're jumping.

2 **What are they doing?**
Look, read, and write.

Andrea

Sam

Hugo

Grace

Alice

1 _____Alice_____ is stretching her body.

2 _____ is stretching his legs.

3 _____ is stretching her arms.

4 Sam is _____ .

5 Grace is _____ .

3 **Who is taking care of their bodies? Look and check (✓).**

4 **How do you take care of your body? Draw and write.**

1 **Talk about what you think happens next in the story.**

I think Oliver plays with the big boys.

I think Oliver plays with Alfie.

2 **Draw the next picture in the story.**

3 **Look at your drawing. Write a conversation.**

Oliver: *Thank you, Alfie.*

Alfie: _____

_____

_____

_____

4 **Act out the conversation.**

Thank you, Alfie.

That's OK.

5 5.37 Listen and check (✓).

1 What does Alfie have?

A  ✓

B

C

2 How old is Amelia?

A

B

C

3 What is Oliver doing now?

A

B

C

4 How is Amelia today?

A

B

C

5 Where's Oliver's skateboard?

A

B

C

6 What would Alfie like to eat?

A

B

C

1 Listen and draw lines. There is one example.

Matt   Nick   Grace   Sam

Tom   May   Eva

1 Play the game.

INSTRUCTIONS

1 Roll the dice and move your marker.
2 Say what the people and animals are doing.

What's he doing?

He's riding a bike.

8 Around the house

My unit goals

Practice	Say and write	Learn to say
	8 **10** **12**	
	new words in English	in English

My mission diary

	Hooray!	OK	Try again
1	😊	😐	😕
2	😊	😐	😕
3	😊	😐	😕
⭐	😊	😐	😕

My favorite stage: _____

Go to page 134 and add to your word stack!

☐ I can name rooms and things in the house.

☐ I can talk about what I can and can't do.

☐ I can listen and color a picture.

☐ I can listen and understand where things are.

1 🎧 5.39 Listen and check (✓) or put an ✗ in the box.

 **X**

Sounds and spelling

2 🎧 5.40 🎧 5.41 Listen and say. Then listen and match.

How do we say this letter?

 living room

 dining room

 lizard

 mirror

 kite

 tiger

 ship

 bike

The Friendly Farm

1 🎧 5.42 **Listen, read, and put a check (✓) or an X in the box.**

1

Rocky can ride a horse. ✓

2

Shelly can't sing. ☐

3

Rocky's brother and sister can't swim. ☐

4

Harry can swim. ☐

5

Rocky can dance. ☐

6

Rocky can eat books. ☐

2 **What can you do? Look and say.**

I can sing, but I can't eat books!

1 Listen and match. Then write.

1 Hugo

2 Sam

3 Pat

4 May

5 Tony

6 Alex

a

b

c

d

e

f

1 _Hugo can play tennis._

2 _____

3 _____

4 _____

5 _____

6 _____

2 Answer the questions. Write *Yes, I can* or *No, I can't.*

All about me

1 *Can you ride a bike?* _____

2 *Can you play the guitar?* _____

3 *Can you swim?* _____

4 *Can you play Ping Pong?* _____

5 *Can you sing?* _____

6 *Can you play soccer?* _____

7 *Can you draw?* _____

8 *Can you ride a horse?* _____

1 **Find and ⟨circle⟩ the words. Then say.**

w	y	s	p	q	s	a	j	l
p	h	o	n	e	t	r	g	b
o	z	f	n	c	m	m	k	e
j	q	a	w	l	e	c	z	d
m	i	r	r	o	r	h	g	v
h	x	u	j	c	l	a	m	p
r	t	g	z	k	g	i	j	r
v	b	l	f	x	o	r	e	q
k	r	p	i	c	t	u	r	e

Number 1 is a picture.

2 **Look at the picture and read the questions. Write one-word answers.**

1 Where is the girl?

on the ___sofa___

2 Who is listening to music?

the _____

3 Where are the girl and boy?

in the _____ room

4 What's the girl doing?

watching _____

5 Where's the boy sitting?

on the _____

6 What color's the wall? _____

7 What's their dad cleaning?

the _____

1 Read and draw lines.

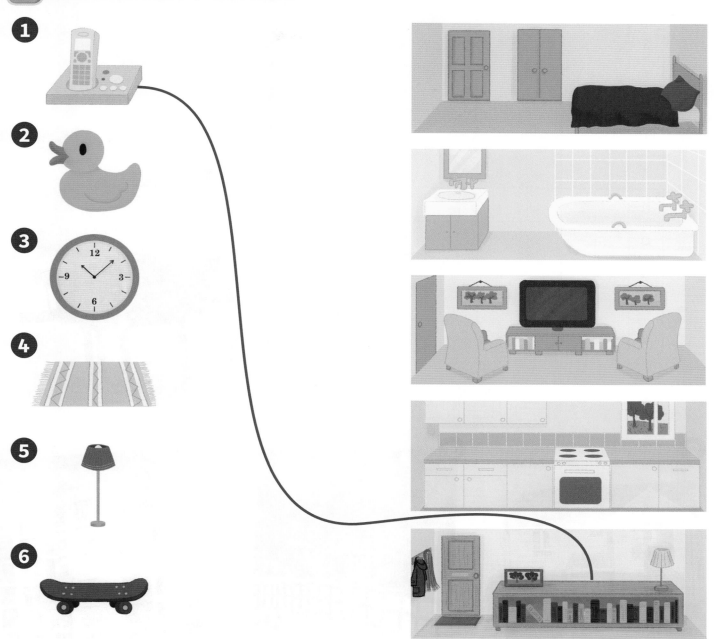

The phone is between the picture and the lamp in the hallway.

The duck is in front of the bathtub in the bathroom.

The clock is in the kitchen. It's between the window and the cupboards.

The rug is on the floor in front of the TV in the living room.

The lamp is behind the armchair in the living room.

The skateboard is in the bedroom. It's between the door and the closet.

1 Write the words.

1 s
t
i
l
t
5 h
o
u
s
e

Learn about different kinds of houses around the world

2 Read and match.

1 I have a treehouse in my yard, and sometimes I sleep there. It's called a treehouse because it's in the trees! In the morning, I can hear the birds. It's great!

2 I live in Vietnam. The houses in my village are lots of different colors, and they are all on the water. I like it because we can swim and catch fish.

3 My house has got four rooms – a living room, a kitchen, a bathroom, and two bedrooms. How is my house different? It moves! I like it because we can go to different places and take our house with us.

3 Think about the house you want to live in. Draw and write.

1 **Read and write the words.**

~~ball~~   bathtub   bounce   clock   OK   table

1 Rob finds a _____ball_____ .

2 Rob and Sue throw and catch and _____ the ball.

3 The ball bounces in the _____ and on the sofa.

4 The ball bounces on the _____ and on the chair.

5 The _____ falls on the mat.

6 Sue says that the clock is _____ .

2 **Sue and Rob play with the ball in the house. That isn't a good idea! What can you do with your friends in the house? What can you do in the yard?**

We can play board games in the house.

We can play soccer in the yard.

3 **Look at the pictures and read the questions. Write one-word answers.**

1   Where are the children?

in Sue's _____ bedroom _____

2   What are they doing?

playing with _____

3   Where is the yellow car?

on the _____

4   What is Rob pointing to?

the red _____

5   Who has the yellow car?

_____

6   Where is the yellow car now?

under the _____

7   Who has the red car?

_____

1 **Listen and color. There is one example.**

1 Play the game.

You're watching TV in the living room. Miss a turn.

a bed ☐
a lamp ☐
an armchair ☐
a phone ☐
a desk ☐
a mat ☐
a cabinet ☐
a picture ☐
a clock ☐
a mirror ☐

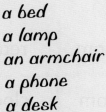

You're singing in the bath. Miss a turn.

Your books are in the bookcase. Roll again.

Your bedroom is clean. Roll again.

What do you have?

I have a lamp for my bedroom.

INSTRUCTIONS

1 Start in the bedroom.

2 Roll the dice and move your marker.

3 Collect all the objects.

4 Go back to your bedroom.

Review •••● Units 7–8

1 Find three words in a line from the same group.

1

watch TV	bathtub	ride a bike
lamp	swim	living room
play soccer	bus stop	kite

2

bed	kitchen	hallway
sofa	ride a horse	kick
armchair	throw	run

3

play tennis	bathroom	read
mirror	bedroom	clock
hit	dining room	rug

4

throw	bathroom	painting
floor	hit	badminton
basketball	dining room	catch

2 Look, read, and write.

arms   body   jumping   legs   running

Look at everyone taking care of their bodies. Hugo is stretching his
_____ . Andrea is stretching her _____ . Alice is
stretching her whole _____ . Grace is _____ high,
and Sam is _____ fast!

3 Read and complete.

1 He's looking in the **roimrr** ___mirror___ .

2 He's brushing his teeth. He's in the **rooabthm** _____ .

3 He's talking to his friend. He's talking on the **oneph** _____ .

4 She's playing tennis. She's got a racket and a **llab** _____ .

4 Read. Then look and correct.

He's ~~playing tennis~~.

___skateboarding___

They like playing basketball.

_____

He's dancing.

_____

She likes reading.

_____

They're catching the balls.

_____

9 Vacation time

My unit goals

Practice	Say and write	Learn to say
	 8 10 12 new words in English	in English

My mission diary

	Hooray!	OK	Try again
1			
2			
3			
★			

My favorite stage: _____

Go to page 134 and add to your word stack!

I can name clothes.

I can understand instructions.

I can talk about things at the beach.

I can read and answer questions about a picture story.

1 Look and read. Write *yes* or *no*.

1

This is a hat.
yes

2

These are socks.

3

These are shoes.

4

This is a skirt.

5

This is a jacket.

6

These are glasses.

7

These are jeans.

8

This is a T-shirt.

Sounds and spelling

2 5.45 Listen and point to the letter.
Then say, match, and write the letter.

j or h?

 j

 h

1

j_eans

2

__and

3

__at

4

__uice

5

__orse

6

__acket

7

__ippo

The Friendly Farm

1 🎧 5.46 **Listen, read, and correct.**

That's Grandpa's new ~~shirt~~!

hat

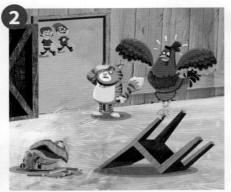

Let's go and eat in the barn.

Come here and pick up these toys, please!

Now clean the mirror, Gracie. It's dirty.

Take those pencils and put them in the box.

Grandpa's hat's there on the sofa.

2 **Act it out with a partner. Say and do. Use the words in the box.**

> pick up   clean   take   put   come

> Pick up those pencils, please.

1 Look, read, and write the number.

1 Anna, pick up that jacket, please.

2 Put the ball in that cabinet there, please.

3 Take this book to the bookcase, please.

4 Pick up those pants, please.

5 Put these bananas on that table, there, please.

6 OK, children, clean these desks, please.

2 Write the words.

boots   ~~read~~   sunglasses   pants

1

Let's ___read___ these books.

2

Are these your _____?

3

Clean those _____.

4

Those aren't your _____.

1 Find and (circle) the words. Then write.

1

shell

2

s	h	e	l	l	q	h	o	p	l	n
j	u	c	v	r	i	s	h	l	n	g
e	z	n	g	b	e	a	c	h	e	l
l	b	n	g	u	w	n	d	a	c	m
l	i	k	w	l	c	d	k	e	r	n
y	t	a	k	e	a	p	h	o	t	o
f	i	s	h	m	m	s	e	a	t	u
i	z	h	k	h	e	t	s	w	s	i
s	u	n	l	t	r	o	y	e	p	g
h	b	o	a	t	a	j	w	b	s	h

9

8

3

4

5

6

7

2 Read and color.

Kim's at the beach. She's sitting on the yellow sand. She has a purple camera, and she's taking a picture of a big pink shell next to her. She has some big green sunglasses on her head. There's an orange boat on the blue sea. It has a big red fish on it. There's a man in the boat. He's fishing.

1 Read and write the words.

The beach

A lot of people like going to the ___beach___ on vacation. You can wear a
(1) _____ and shorts, and you can do different things there.

Some people enjoy sitting in the sun, reading a book, or listening to the
(2) _____ . Children like playing on the sand. They can pick up
(3) _____ and write their names with them.

A lot of people enjoy swimming in the **(4)** _____ . They can look at
(5) _____ and shells under the water.

beach   **sea**   **boots**   **radio**

camera   **fish**   **shells**   **T-shirt**

1 **Write the words.**

beach   forest   mountains   ~~river~~

1

2

river

3

4

2 **Draw a landscape from Activity 1.**
Draw and label four things you can see there.

3 Read the postcard and write the words.

Dear Mark,

I'm on vacation with my family in Australia. It's amazing! We are staying in a [house image] ¹ _house_

in the forest. There are lots of

[birds image] ² _____ in the

[trees image] ³ _____ . There are beautiful

[flowers image] ⁴ _____ , too. We can't pick

them, but we can take [pictures image] ⁵ _____

of them. We can ride our [bicycle image] ⁶ _____

every day. We can ride horses, too. It's really fun!

See you soon,

Hugo

4 Read again and write yes or no.

1   Hugo is in Australia.   _yes_

2   Hugo is enjoying his vacation.   _____

3   The house is at the beach.   _____

4   There are birds and trees.   _____

5   They can take pictures of the flowers.   _____

6   Hugo likes riding horses.   _____

1 **Number the pictures in order. Then tell the story.**

The monkey gives coconuts to the shark.

2 **Imagine you are the monkey or the shark in the story. What do you do next? Draw a picture. Write about your picture.**

3 🎧 5.47 Listen and color.

4 Ask and answer.

What are these?
Do you eat coconuts?
What do you eat for lunch?

What's this?
Do you eat fish?
What do you eat for dinner?

What are these? They're coconuts.

What's this?
Do you like monkeys?
What pet would you like to have?

What's this?
Can you swim?
What do you do on vacation?

1 **Look at the pictures and read the questions. Write one-word answers.**

Examples

How many children are there?
_____ 3 _____

What does the boy have on his head? a _____ hat _____

Questions

1 What is the girl with the green skirt doing?
listening to _____

2 Which animal is next to the flower? _____

3 What is the boy eating?
_____

4 What are the girls doing?
_____

5 Where is the spider now?
on the _____

1 Play the game.

START

You're wearing a sunhat. Roll again.

You haven't got your sunhat. Miss a turn.

You can't find your sunglasses. Miss a turn.

You're taking a nice picture of your mom and dad. Roll again.

FINISH

They like playing at the beach.

She doesn't like the purple dress.

INSTRUCTIONS

1   Roll the dice and move your marker.
2   Say what the people like or don't like.

10 Review Unit
Units 1–3

1 **Write *in*, *on*, or *next to*.**

1

The table is _____ the classroom.

2

The colored pencils are _____ the desk.

3

The chair is _____ the table.

2 **Write the sentence in the correct order.**

the / next to / ruler / crayons / The / are / .

_____

_____

3 **Look, match, and write.**

a   This is Mrs. Friendly.

She's Jim and Jenny's _____.

b   This is Jenny.

She's Jim's _____.

c   This is Mr. Friendly.

He's Jim and Jenny's *father*.

d   This is Jim.

He's Jenny's _____.

4 **Look and write *has* or *have*.**

1   This horse _____
a gray head.

2   These cats _____
orange ears.

3   This dog _____
black and white legs.

4   These chickens _____
brown bodies.

5 🎧 5.48 Listen and number. Then match and write.

1   It has <u>white</u> fur and a <u>short</u> tail.

2   _____ has _____ hair and _____ eyes.

3   _____ has _____ hair and _____ eyes.

6 Choose an adjective and an animal. Make a sentence and act it out for your partner to guess.

Adjectives	Animals
angry **happy** **young** sad old **funny**	**horse** chicken **duck** **cow** goat **sheep**

Yes, I am!

Are you a funny duck?

7 Write

ACROSS:

A–1 He is Jim and Jenny's _grandfather_.

A–2 A _____ has four legs.

A–3 I smell with my _____.

A–4 Jim and Jenny are _____.

1 g r a n d f a t h e r

DOWN:

D–1 Gracie is a _____.

D–2 Do you have a _____?

D–3 I eat with my _____.

D–4 I like to color with _____.

1 🎧 5.49 **What does Eva like? Listen and put a check (✓) or an ✗ in the box.**

1

☐   ☐   ☐

2

☐   ☐   ☐

3

☐   ☐   ☐

2 **Look at Activity 1. Ask and answer questions.**

What does Eva like?

She likes _____, _____, and _____.

3 **Look and write.**

Jim's   Jim and Jenny's   Jenny's

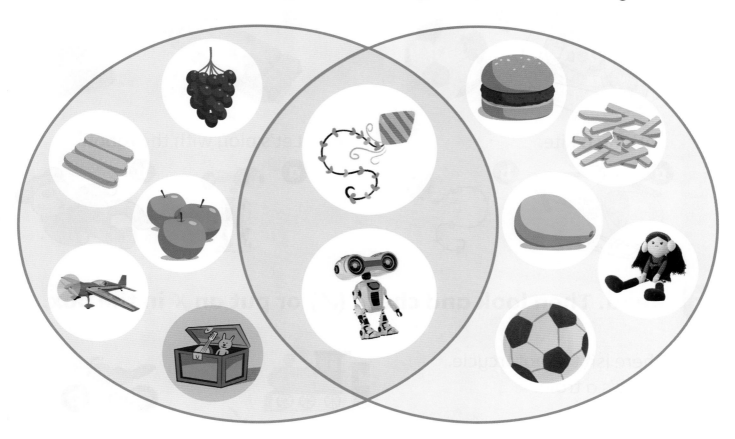

1 What are Jim's toys?

His toys are the pl _ _ _ and the t _ y _ ox.

2 What are Jenny's toys?

Her toys are the d _ _ _ and the _ all.

3 Look at the apples and sausages. Whose food is this?

It's _ _ _ 's food.

4 Look at the hamburger and french fries. Whose food is this?

It's _ _ _ _ _ 's food.

5 Look at the kite and the robot. Are these Jim and Jenny's?

Yes. These are _ _ eir toys.

4 Read and (circle) the correct picture.

1 Let's play a board game.

a 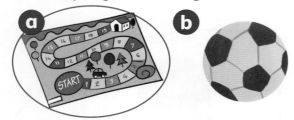 b

2 Let's fly a kite.

a 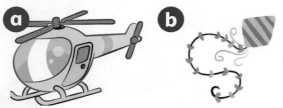 b

3 Let's have some cake.

a 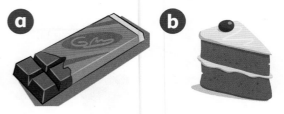 b

4 Let's play with the robot.

a  b

5 Read. Then look and check (✓) or put an ✗ in the box.

1 There isn't a motorcycle.
There's a train.

 ✓    ✗

2 There isn't a tree.
There are flowers.

 ☐    ☐

3 There aren't any cars.
There is a bus.

 ☐    ☐

4 There isn't a lion.
There's a tiger.

 ☐    ☐

6 **Find and ⟨circle⟩ the words. Then ask and answer with a partner.**

~~bananas~~ bread fruit grapes juice
lemonade mango pasta salad sausage

B	A	N	A	N	A	S	J	Z	M
R	P	A	S	T	A	A	U	Y	A
E	T	S	P	F	R	U	I	T	N
A	S	A	L	A	D	S	C	R	G
D	M	N	E	O	P	A	E	Q	O
L	K	J	I	H	G	G	F	E	E
B	A	G	R	A	P	E	S	Z	S
W	L	E	M	O	N	A	D	E	X

Do you like bananas?

Yes, I do.

1 🎧 5.50 **Listen and number.**

2 **Look at Activity 1. Use words from the box and write two sentences.**

> boy   girl   mother   father   grandfather   ~~baby~~   playing guitar
> eating an orange   ~~drinking a bottle~~   listening to music

The baby is drinking a bottle.

1 _____

2 _____

3 **Look at Activity 1. Ask and answer with a partner.**

> The girl's riding a bike.
> Can you ride a bike?

> Yes, I can.
> The father's playing guitar.
> Can you play the guitar?

> No, I can't.

4 **Look, read, and (circle.)**

1   Jim's **watching television** / **playing the piano.**

2   Eva's **reading a book** / **drawing a picture.**

3   Grandma's **drinking water** / **eating an apple.**

4   Jenny's **listening to music** / **playing the violin.**

5   Mr. Friendly's **looking in the mirror** / **brushing his teeth.**

6   Grandpa's **cleaning the floor** / **cleaning the table.**

5   **Where are they? Write.**

1   Where is Jim?

He's in the living room.

2   Where is Jenny?

She's _____

3   Where is Grandma?

_____

6 Write.

sneakers   sunglasses   hat   shorts

1   Put your _____ over there, please.

2   Put the _____ away, please.

3   Pick up those _____, please.

4   Clean those _____, please.

7 Draw a messy room. Show your picture to a partner. Take turns telling your partner what to do.

Put your clothes away, please.

OK.

8 Find your way to the beach. Read and (circle) the pictures.

When my family goes to the beach, …

1 I like taking pictures with a **camera**.
2 My sister likes picking up **shells**.
3 My brother enjoys listening to his **radio**.
4 My mom likes swimming in the **sea**.
5 My dad enjoys catching **fish**.
6 My grandma likes wearing **sunglasses**.

This way to the Beach →

The Beach

9 What do you like to do at the beach? Ask and answer with a partner.

What do you like to do?

I like to listen to music. What do you like to do?

I like to pick up shells.

1 Write your favorite new words.

WORD STACK